THE ORDER OF HOLY MASS

WITH ALL PREFACE PRAYERS

Corpus Christi Publishing

Corpus Christi Publishing
4649 Parrish Avenue
Salina, CA 93901
California
USA

Copyright © 2020 Corpus Christi Publishing
All rights reserved. No part of this publication may be stored in a retrieval system, transmitted or reproduced in any way, including but not limited to photocopy, photograph, magnetic or other record, without the prior agreement and written permission of the publisher.

CONTENTS

SECTION I
ORDER OF MASS

THE INTRODUCTORY RITES.............................2

The Penitential Act...3

The Kyrie Eleison..5

The Gloria..5

The Collect (Opening Prayer)...........................6

THE LITURGY OF THE WORD........................6

The Credo (Profession of Faith).......................8

THE LITURGY OF THE EUCHARIST...............9

Eucharistic Prayer I...11

Eucharistic Prayer II..17

Eucharistic Prayer III.......................................21

Eucharistic Prayer IV......................................25

THE COMMUNION RITES.............................31

Breaking of the Bread.....................................32

Communion...33

Prayer after Communion................................33

THE CONCLUDING RITES...........................34

Dismissal..34

SECTION II
PREFACES OF HOLY MASS

PREFACE I OF ADVENT..............................37

PREFACE II OF ADVENT............................37

PREFACE I OF THE NATIVITY
OF THE LORD..38

PREFACE II OF THE NATIVITY
OF THE LORD..38

PREFACE III OF THE NATIVITY
OF THE LORD..39

EPIPHANY OF THE LORD.........................39

PREFACE OF LENT I.................................40

PREFACE OF LENT II................................41

PREFACE OF LENT III...............................41

PREFACE OF LENT IV...............................42

PREFACE I OF THE PASSION
OF THE LORD..42

PREFACE II OF THE PASSION
OF THE LORD..43

PREFACE I OF EASTER.............................43

PREFACE II OF EASTER............................44

PREFACE III OF EASTER...........................44

PREFACE IV OF EASTER...........................45

PREFACE V OF EASTER..................................46

PREFACE I OF THE ASCENSION
OF THE LORD..46

PREFACE II OF THE ASCENSION
OF THE LORD..47

PREFACE I OF THE SUNDAYS
IN ORDINARY TIME....................................48

PREFACE II OF THE SUNDAYS
IN ORDINARY TIME....................................48

PREFACE III OF THE SUNDAYS
IN ORDINARY TIME....................................49

PREFACE IV OF THE SUNDAYS
IN ORDINARY TIME....................................50

PREFACE V OF THE SUNDAYS
IN ORDINARY TIME....................................50

PREFACE VI OF THE SUNDAYS
IN ORDINARY TIME....................................51

PREFACE VII OF THE SUNDAYS
IN ORDINARY TIME....................................51

PREFACE VIII OF THE SUNDAYS
IN ORDINARY TIME....................................52

PREFACE I OF THE MOST HOLY
EUCHARIST...52

PREFACE II OF THE MOST HOLY
EUCHARIST..53
PREFACE I OF THE BLESSED
VIRGIN MARY..54
PREFACE II OF THE BLESSED
VIRGIN MARY..54
PREFACE I OF THE APOSTLES...................55
PREFACE II OF THE APOSTLES..................56
PREFACE I OF SAINTS.............................56
PREFACE II OF SAINTS............................57
PREFACE I OF HOLY MARTYRS..................58
PREFACE II OF HOLY MARTYRS.................58
PREFACE OF HOLY PASTORS.....................59
PREFACE OF HOLY VIRGINS
AND RELIGIOUS......................................60
COMMON PREFACE I................................60
COMMON PREFACE II...............................61
COMMON PREFACE III..............................62
COMMON PREFACE IV..............................62
COMMON PREFACE V...............................63
COMMON PREFACE VI..............................63
PREFACE I FOR THE DEAD........................64
PREFACE II FOR THE DEAD.......................65

PREFACE III FOR THE DEAD......................65

PREFACE IV FOR THE DEAD......................66

PREFACE V FOR THE DEAD.......................66

Eternal rest grant unto them O Lord, and let perpetual light shine upon them, May they rest in peace.
Amen

SECTION I
ORDER OF MASS

THE INTRODUCTORY RITES

When the people are gathered, the Priest (P:) approaches the altar with the altar servers while the Entrance Chant is sung. When he has arrived at the altar, after making a profound bow with the altar servers, the Priest venerates the altar with a kiss and, if appropriate, incenses the cross and the altar. As the Entrance Chant is concluded, the Priest and the Congregation (C:), standing, make the sign of the cross as the Priest, facing the people, says:

P: In the name of the Father, and of the Son, and of the Holy Spirit.

C: Amen.

Then the Priest, extending his hands, greets the people, saying:

P: The grace of our Lord Jesus Christ, and the love of God, and the communion of the Holy Spirit be with you all.

Or:

P: Grace to you and peace from God our Father and the Lord Jesus Christ.

Or:

P: The Lord be with you.

(Or a Bishop (B:) says: Peace be with you).

C: And with your spirit.

The Penitential Act

Form A

P: Brethren (brothers and sisters), let us acknowledge our sins, and so prepare ourselves to celebrate the sacred mysteries.

A brief pause for silence follows. Then all recite together the formula of general confession:

I confess to almighty God and to you my brothers and sisters, that I have greatly sinned, in my thoughts and in my words, in what I have done and in what I have failed to do,

And, striking their breast, they say:

Through my fault, through my fault, through my most grievous fault,

Then they continue:

Therefore I ask blessed Mary ever Virgin, all the Angels and Saints, and you, my brothers and sisters, to pray for me to the Lord our God.

The absolution of the Priest follows:

P: May almighty God have mercy on us, forgive us our sins, and bring us to everlasting life

C: Amen.

Or: Form B

P: Brethren (brothers and sisters), let us acknowledge our sins, and so prepare ourselves to celebrate the sacred mysteries.

A brief pause for silence follows. Then

P: Have mercy on us, O Lord.

C: For we have sinned against you.

P: Show us, O Lord, your mercy.

C: And grant us your salvation.

P: May almighty God have mercy on us, forgive us our sins, and bring us to everlasting life.

C: Amen.

Or: Form C

P: Brethren (brothers and sisters), let us acknowledge our sins, and so prepare ourselves to celebrate the sacred mysteries.

A brief pause for silence follows.

P: You were sent to heal the contrite of heart: Lord, have mercy.

C: Lord, have mercy.

P: You came to call sinners: Christ, have mercy.

C: Christ, have mercy.

P: You are seated at the right hand of the Father to intercede for us: Lord, have mercy.

C: Lord, have mercy.

P: May almighty God have mercy on us, forgive us our sins, and bring us to everlasting life.

C: Amen.

The Kyrie Eleison

The Kyrie eleison (Lord, have mercy) invocations follow, unless they have just occurred in a formula of the Penitential Act.

P. Lord, have mercy.

C. Lord, have mercy.

P. Christ, have mercy.

C. Christ, have mercy.

P. Lord, have mercy.

C. Lord, have mercy.

The Gloria

(Omitted during Lent, Advent and Mass for the dead)

Then, when it is prescribed, this hymn is either sung or said:

Glory to God in the highest, and on earth peace to people of good will. We praise you, we bless you, we adore you, we glorify you, we give you thanks for your great glory. Lord God, heavenly King. O God, almighty Father. Lord Jesus Christ, Only Begotten Son, Lord God, Lamb of God, Son of the Father, You take away the sins of the world. Have mercy on us; you take away the sins of the world, receive our prayer; You are seated at the right hand of the Father, have mercy on us. For you alone are the Holy One, you alone are the Lord, you alone are the Most High, Jesus Christ, with the Holy Spirit, In the glory of God the Father. Amen.

The Collect (Opening Prayer)

P: Let us pray.

And all pray in silence with the Priest for a while.

Then the Priest, with hands extended, says the Collect prayer, at the end of which the people acclaim:

C: Amen.

THE LITURGY OF THE WORD

The Reader (R:) goes to the ambo and reads the First Reading, while all sit and listen. To indicate the end of the reading, the reader acclaims:

R: The word of the Lord.

C: Thanks be to God.

This is followed by the psalmist or cantor who sings or says the Psalm, with the people making the response. After this, if there is to be a Second Reading, the reader reads it from the ambo, as above. To indicate the end of the reading, the reader acclaims:

R: The word of the Lord.

C: Thanks be to God.

There follows the Alleluia, as the liturgical time requires Meanwhile, if incense is used, the Priest puts some into the thurible. After this, the Deacon (D:) who is to proclaim the Gospel, bowing profoundly before the Priest, asks for the blessing, saying in a low voice:

D: Your blessing, Father.

The Priest says in a low voice:

P: May the Lord be in your heart and on your lips, that you may proclaim His Gospel worthily and well, in the name of the Father and of the Son and of the Holy Spirit.

The Deacon makes the Sign of the Cross and replies:

D: Amen.

If, however, a Deacon is not present, the Priest, bowing before the altar, says quietly:

P: Cleanse my heart and my lips, almighty God, that I may worthily proclaim your holy Gospel.

The Deacon, or the Priest, then proceeds to the ambo, accompanied, if appropriate, by altar servers with incense and candles.

P: The Lord be with you.

C: And with your spirit.

The Deacon, or the Priest:

A reading from the holy Gospel according to N.

And, at the same time, he makes the Sign of the Cross on the book and on his forehead, lips, and breast.

C: Glory to you, O Lord.

Then the Deacon, or the Priest, incenses the book, if incense is used, and proclaims the Gospel. At the end of the Gospel, the Deacon, or the Priest, acclaims:

P: The Gospel of the Lord.

C: Praise to you, Lord Jesus Christ.

Then he (the Deacon or the Priest) kisses the book, saying quietly:

P: Through the words of the Gospel may our sins be wiped away.

Then follows the Homily, which is to be preached by a Priest or Deacon.

The Credo (Profession of Faith)
The Nicene Creed

I believe in one God, The Father almighty, Maker of heaven and earth, of all things visible and invisible. I believe in one Lord Jesus Christ, The Only Begotten Son of God, born of the Father before all ages. God from God, Light from Light, True God from true God, Begotten, not made, Consubstantial with the Father; Through him all things were made. For us men and for our salvation He came down from heaven, and by the Holy Spirit was incarnate of the Virgin Mary, and became man. For our sake He was crucified under Pontius Pilate, He suffered death and was buried, And rose again on the third day In accordance with the Scriptures. He ascended into heaven and is seated At the right hand of the Father. He will come again in glory To judge the living and the dead And his kingdom will have no end. I believe in the Holy Spirit, the Lord, the giver of life, Who proceeds from the Father and the Son, Who with the Father and the Son is adored and glorified, Who has spoken through the prophets. I believe in one, holy, catholic and apostolic Church. I confess one Baptism for the forgiveness of sins And I look forward to the resurrection of the dead And the life of the world to come. Amen.

The Apostles' Creed

Instead of the Nicene Creed, especially during Lent and Easter Time, the Apostles' Creed, may be used.

I believe in God, the Father almighty, Creator of heaven and earth, And in Jesus Christ, his only Son, our Lord, Who was conceived by the Holy Spirit, Born of the Virgin Mary, Suffered under Pontius Pilate, Was crucified, died and was buried; He descended into hell; On the third day he rose again from the dead; He ascended into heaven, And is seated at the right hand of God the Father almighty; From there he will come to judge the living and the dead. I believe in the Holy Spirit, The holy Catholic Church, The communion of saints, The forgiveness of sins, The resurrection of the body, And life everlasting. Amen.

THE LITURGY OF THE EUCHARIST

The Priest, standing at the altar, takes the paten with the bread and holds it slightly raised above the altar with both hands, saying in a low voice:

P: Blessed are you, Lord God of all creation, for through your goodness we have received the bread we offer you: fruit of the earth and work of human hands, it will become for us the bread of life.

Then he places the paten with the bread on the corporal.

The people may acclaim:

C: Blessed be God for ever.

The Priest, pours wine and a little water into the chalice, saying quietly:

P: By the mystery of this water and wine, may we come to share in the divinity of Christ who humbled himself to share in our humanity.

The Priest then takes the chalice and holds it slightly raised above the altar with both hands, saying in a low voice:

P: Blessed are you, Lord God of all creation, for through your goodness we have received the wine we offer you: fruit of the vine and work of human hands, it will become our spiritual drink.

Then he places the chalice on the corporal.

C: Blessed be God for ever.

After this, the Priest, bowing profoundly, says quietly:

P: With humble spirit and contrite heart may we be accepted by you, O Lord, and may our sacrifice in your sight this day be pleasing to you, Lord God.

Then the Priest, standing at the side of the altar, washes his hands, saying quietly:

P: Wash me, O Lord, from my iniquity and cleanse me from my sin.

Standing at the middle of the altar, facing the people, extending and then joining his hands, he says:

P: Pray, brethren (brothers and sisters), that my sacrifice and yours may be acceptable to God, the almighty Father.

The people rise and reply:

C: May the Lord accept the sacrifice at your hands for the praise and glory of his name, for our good and the good of all his holy Church.

Then the Priest, with hands extended, says the Prayer over the Gifts, at the end of which the people acclaim:

C: Amen.

Eucharistic Prayer I

P: The Lord be with you.

C: And with your spirit.

P: Lift up your hearts.

C: We lift them up to the Lord.

P: Let us give thanks to the Lord our God.

C: It is right and just.

The Priest continues with the Preface to be used in accord with the rubrics (see SECTION II), which concludes:

Holy, Holy, Holy Lord God of hosts. Heaven and earth are full of your glory. Hosanna in the highest. Blessed is he who comes in the name of the Lord. Hosanna in the highest.

The Priest, with hands extended, says:

P: To you, therefore, most merciful Father, we make humble prayer and petition through Jesus Christ, your Son, our Lord:

He joins his hands and says

P: that you accept

He makes the Sign of the Cross once over the bread and chalice together, saying:

P: and bless these gifts, these offerings, these holy and unblemished sacrifices,

With hands extended, he continues:

P: which we offer you firstly for your holy Catholic Church. Be pleased to grant her peace, to guard, unite and govern her throughout the whole world, together with your servant N. our Pope and N. our Bishop, and all those who, holding to the truth, hand on the catholic and apostolic faith.

Commemoration of the Living

P: Remember, Lord, your servants N. and N.

The Priest joins his hands and prays briefly for those for whom he intends to pray. Then, with hands extended, he continues:

P: and all gathered here, whose faith and devotion are known to you. For them, we offer you this sacrifice of praise or they offer it for themselves and all who are dear to them: for the redemption of their souls, in hope of health and well-being, and paying their homage to you, the eternal God, living and true.

In communion with those whose memory we venerate, especially the glorious ever-Virgin Mary, Mother of our God and Lord, Jesus Christ, and blessed Joseph, her Spouse, your blessed Apostles and Martyrs, Peter and Paul, Andrew, (James, John, Thomas, James, Philip, Bartholomew, Matthew, Simon and Jude; Linus, Cletus, Clement, Sixtus, Cornelius, Cyprian, Lawrence, Chrysogonus, John and Paul, Cosmas and Damian) and all your Saints; we ask that through their merits and prayers, in all things we may be defended by your protecting help. (Through Christ our Lord. Amen.)

With hands extended, the Priest continues:

P: Therefore, Lord, we pray: graciously accept this oblation of our service, that of your whole family; order our days in your peace, and command that we be delivered from eternal damnation and counted among the flock of those you have chosen. (Through Christ our Lord. Amen.)

Holding his hands extended over the offerings, he says:

P: Be pleased, O God, we pray, to bless, acknowledge, and approve this offering in every respect; make it spiritual and acceptable, so that it may become for us the Body and Blood of your most beloved Son, our Lord Jesus Christ.

He joins his hands.

P: On the day before he was to suffer,

He takes the bread and, holding it slightly raised above the altar, continues:

P: he took bread in his holy and venerable hands, and with eyes raised to heaven to you, O God, his almighty Father, giving you thanks, he said the blessing, broke the bread and gave it to his disciples, saying:

He bows slightly.

P: TAKE THIS, ALL OF YOU, AND EAT OF IT, FOR THIS IS MY BODY, WHICH WILL BE GIVEN UP FOR YOU.

He shows the consecrated host to the people, places it again on the paten, and genuflects in adoration.

P: In a similar way, when supper was ended,

He takes the chalice and, holding it slightly raised above the altar, continues:

P: he took this precious chalice in his holy and venerable hands, and once more giving you thanks, he said the blessing and gave the chalice to his disciples, saying:

He bows slightly.

P: TAKE THIS, ALL OF YOU, AND DRINK FROM IT, FOR THIS IS THE CHALICE OF MY BLOOD, THE BLOOD OF THE NEW AND ETERNAL COVENANT, WHICH WILL BE POURED OUT FOR YOU AND FOR MANY FOR THE FORGIVENESS OF SINS. DO THIS IN MEMORY OF ME.

He shows the chalice to the people, places it on the corporal, and genuflects in adoration. Then he says:

P: The mystery of faith.

C: We proclaim your Death, O Lord, and profess your Resurrection until you come again.

Or:

When we eat this Bread and drink this Cup, we proclaim your Death, O Lord, until you come again.

Or:

Save us, Savior of the world, for by your Cross and Resurrection you have set us free.

Then the Priest, with hands extended, says:

P: Therefore, O Lord, as we celebrate the memorial of the blessed Passion, the Resurrection from the dead, and the glorious Ascension into heaven of Christ, your Son, our Lord, we, your servants and your holy people, offer to your glorious majesty from the gifts that you have given us, this pure victim, this holy victim, this spotless victim, the holy Bread of eternal life and the Chalice of everlasting salvation.

Be pleased to look upon these offerings with a serene and kindly countenance, and to accept them, as once you were pleased to accept the gifts of your servant Abel the just, the sacrifice of Abraham, our father in faith, and the offering of your high priest Melchizedek, a holy sacrifice, a spotless victim.

Bowing, with hands joined, he continues:

P: In humble prayer we ask you, almighty God: command that these gifts be borne by the hands of your holy Angel to your altar on high in the sight of your divine majesty, so that all of us, who through this participation at the altar receive the most holy Body and Blood of your Son,

He stands upright again and makes the Sign of the Cross, saying:

P: may be filled with every grace and heavenly blessing. (Through Christ our Lord. Amen.)

Commemoration of the Dead

With hands extended, the Priest says:

P: Remember also, Lord, your servants N. and N., who have gone before us with the sign of faith and rest in the sleep of peace.

He joins his hands and prays briefly for those who have died and for whom he intends to pray. Then, with hands extended, he continues:

P: Grant them, O Lord, we pray, and all who sleep in Christ, a place of refreshment, light and peace. (Through Christ our Lord. Amen.)

He strikes his breast with his right hand, saying:

P: To us, also, your servants, who, though sinners,

And, with hands extended, he continues:

P: hope in your abundant mercies, graciously grant some share and fellowship with your holy Apostles and Martyrs: with John the Baptist, Stephen, Matthias, Barnabas, (Ignatius, Alexander,

Marcellinus, Peter, Felicity, Perpetua, Agatha, Lucy, Agnes, Cecilia, Anastasia) and all your Saints; admit us, we beseech you, into their company, not weighing our merits, but granting us your pardon, through Christ our Lord.

And he continues:

P: Through whom you continue to make all these good things, O Lord; you sanctify them, fill them with life, bless them, and bestow them upon us.

He takes the chalice and the paten with the host and, raising both, he says:

P: Through him, and with him, and in him, O God, almighty Father, in the unity of the Holy Spirit, all glory and honor is yours, for ever and ever.

C: Amen.

Then follows the Communion Rite

Eucharistic Prayer II

P: The Lord be with you.

C: And with your spirit.

P: Lift up your hearts.

C: We lift them up to the Lord.

P: Let us give thanks to the Lord our God.

C: It is right and just.

The Priest continues with the Preface to be used in accord with the rubrics (see SECTION II), which concludes:

Holy, Holy, Holy Lord God of hosts. Heaven and earth are full of your glory. Hosanna in the highest. Blessed is he who comes in the name of the Lord. Hosanna in the highest.

The Priest, with hands extended, says:

P: You are indeed Holy, O Lord, the fount of all holiness.

He joins his hands and, holding them extended over the offerings, says:

P: Make holy, therefore, these gifts, we pray, by sending down your Spirit upon them like the dewfall,

He joins his hands and makes the Sign of the Cross once over the bread and the chalice together, saying:

P: so that they may become for us the Body and Blood of our Lord Jesus Christ.

He joins his hands.

P: At the time he was betrayed and entered willingly into his Passion,

He takes the bread and, holding it slightly raised above the altar, continues:

P: he took bread and, giving thanks, broke it, and gave it to his disciples, saying:

He bows slightly.

P: TAKE THIS, ALL OF YOU, AND EAT OF IT, FOR THIS IS MY BODY, WHICH WILL BE GIVEN UP FOR YOU.

He shows the consecrated host to the people, places it again on the paten, and genuflects in adoration. After this, he continues:

P: In a similar way, when supper was ended,

He takes the chalice and, holding it slightly raised above the altar, continues:

P: he took the chalice and, once more giving thanks, he gave it to his disciples, saying:

He bows slightly.

P: TAKE THIS, ALL OF YOU, AND DRINK FROM IT, FOR THIS IS THE CHALICE OF MY BLOOD, THE BLOOD OF THE NEW AND ETERNAL COVENANT, WHICH WILL BE POURED OUT FOR YOU AND FOR MANY FOR THE FORGIVENESS OF SINS. DO THIS IN MEMORY OF ME.

He shows the chalice to the people, places it on the corporal, and genuflects in adoration. Then he says:

P: The mystery of faith.

C: We proclaim your Death,

O Lord, and profess your Resurrection until you come again.

Or:

When we eat this Bread and drink this Cup, we proclaim your Death, O Lord, until you come again.

Or:

Save us, Savior of the world, for by your Cross and Resurrection you have set us free.

Then the Priest, with hands extended, says:

P: Therefore, as we celebrate the memorial of his Death and Resurrection, we offer you, Lord, the Bread of life and the Chalice of salvation, giving thanks that you have held us worthy to be in your presence and minister to you.

Humbly we pray that, partaking of the Body and Blood of Christ, we may be gathered into one by the Holy Spirit. Remember, Lord, your Church, spread throughout the world, and bring her to the fullness of charity, together with N. our Pope and N. our Bishop, and all the clergy.

Remember also our brothers and sisters who have fallen asleep in the hope of the resurrection, and all who have died in your mercy: welcome them into the light of your face. Have mercy on us all, we pray, that with the Blessed Virgin Mary, Mother of God, with the blessed Apostles, and all the Saints who have pleased you throughout the ages, we may merit to be coheirs to eternal life, and may praise and glorify you through your Son, Jesus Christ.

He takes the chalice and the paten with the host and, raising both, he says:

P: Through him, and with him, and in him, O God, almighty Father, in the unity of the Holy Spirit, all glory and honor is yours, for ever and ever.

C: Amen.

Then follows the Communion Rite

Eucharistic Prayer III

P: The Lord be with you.

C: And with your spirit.

P: Lift up your hearts.

C: We lift them up to the Lord.

P: Let us give thanks to the Lord our God.

C: It is right and just.

The Priest continues with the Preface to be used in accord with the rubrics (see SECTION II), which concludes:

Holy, Holy, Holy Lord God of hosts. Heaven and earth are full of your glory. Hosanna in the highest. Blessed is he who comes in the name of the Lord. Hosanna in the highest.

The Priest, with hands extended, says:

P: You are indeed Holy, O Lord, and all you have created rightly gives you praise, for through your Son our Lord Jesus Christ, by the power and working of the Holy Spirit, you give life to all things and make them holy, and you never cease to gather a people to yourself, so that from the rising of the sun to its setting a pure sacrifice may be offered to your name.

He joins his hands and, holding them extended over the offerings, says:
P: Therefore, O Lord, we humbly implore you: by the same Spirit graciously make holy these gifts we have brought to you for consecration,

He joins his hands and makes the Sign of the Cross once over the bread and chalice together, saying:
P: that they may become the Body and Blood of your Son our Lord Jesus Christ,

He joins his hands.
P: at whose command we celebrate these mysteries. For on the night he was betrayed

He takes the bread and, holding it slightly raised above the altar, continues:
P: he himself took bread, and, giving you thanks, he said the blessing, broke the bread and gave it to his disciples, saying:

He bows slightly
P: TAKE THIS, ALL OF YOU, AND EAT OF IT, FOR THIS IS MY BODY, WHICH WILL BE GIVEN UP FOR YOU.

He shows the consecrated host to the people, places it again on the paten, and genuflects in adoration. After this, he continues:
P: In a similar way, when supper was ended,

He takes the chalice and, holding it slightly raised above the altar, continues:

P: he took the chalice, and, giving you thanks, he said the blessing, and gave the chalice to his disciples, saying:

He bows slightly.

P: TAKE THIS, ALL OF YOU, AND DRINK FROM IT, FOR THIS IS THE CHALICE OF MY BLOOD, THE BLOOD OF THE NEW AND ETERNAL COVENANT, WHICH WILL BE POURED OUT FOR YOU AND FOR MANY FOR THE FORGIVENESS OF SINS. DO THIS IN MEMORY OF ME.

He shows the chalice to the people, places it on the corporal, and genuflects in adoration. Then he says:

P: The mystery of faith.

C: We proclaim your Death, O Lord, and profess your Resurrection until you come again.

Or:

When we eat this Bread and drink this Cup, we proclaim your Death, O Lord, until you come again.

Or:

Save us, Savior of the world, for by your Cross and Resurrection you have set us free.

Then the Priest, with hands extended, says:

P: Therefore, O Lord, as we celebrate the memorial of the saving Passion of your Son, his wondrous Resurrection and Ascension into heaven, and as we look forward to his second coming, we offer you in thanksgiving this holy and living sacrifice.

Look, we pray, upon the oblation of your Church and, recognizing the sacrificial Victim by whose death you willed to reconcile us to yourself, grant that we, who are nourished by the Body and Blood of your Son and filled with his Holy Spirit, may become one body, one spirit in Christ.

May he make of us an eternal offering to you, so that we may obtain an inheritance with your elect, especially with the most Blessed Virgin Mary, Mother of God, with blessed Joseph, her Spouse, with your blessed Apostles and glorious Martyrs (with Saint N.: the Saint of the day or Patron Saint) and with all the Saints, on whose constant intercession in your presence we rely for unfailing help.

May this Sacrifice of our reconciliation, we pray, O Lord, advance the peace and salvation of all the world. Be pleased to confirm in faith and charity your pilgrim Church on earth, with your servant N. our Pope and N. our Bishop, the Order of Bishops, all the clergy, and the entire people you have gained for your own.

Listen graciously to the prayers of this family, whom you have summoned before you: in your compassion, O merciful Father, gather to yourself all your children scattered throughout the world.

To our departed brothers and sisters and to all who were pleasing to you at their passing from this life, give kind admittance to your kingdom. There we hope to enjoy for ever the fullness of your glory through Christ our Lord, through whom you bestow on the world all that is good.

He takes the chalice and the paten with the host and, raising both, he says:

P: Through him, and with him, and in him, O God, almighty Father, in the unity of the Holy Spirit, all glory and honor is yours, for ever and ever.

C: Amen.

Then follows the Communion Rite

Eucharistic Prayer IV

P: The Lord be with you.

C: And with your spirit.

P: Lift up your hearts.

C: We lift them up to the Lord.

P: Let us give thanks to the Lord our God.

C: It is right and just.

The Priest continues with the Preface to be used in accord with the rubrics (see SECTION II), which concludes:

C: Holy, Holy, Holy Lord God of hosts. Heaven and earth are full of your glory. Hosanna in the highest. Blessed is he who comes in the name of the Lord. Hosanna in the highest.

The Priest, with hands extended, says:

P: We give you praise, Father most holy, for you are great and you have fashioned all your works in wisdom and in love. You formed man in your own image and entrusted the whole world to his care, so that in serving you alone, the Creator, he might have dominion over all creatures.

And when through disobedience he had lost your friendship, you did not abandon him to the domain of death. For you came in mercy to the aid of all, so that those who seek might find you. Time and again you offered them covenants and through the prophets taught them to look forward to salvation.

And you so loved the world, Father most holy, that in the fullness of time you sent your Only Begotten Son to be our Savior. Made incarnate by the Holy Spirit and born of the Virgin Mary, he shared our human nature in all things but sin. To the poor he proclaimed the good news of salvation, to prisoners, freedom, and to the sorrowful of heart, joy. To accomplish your plan, he gave himself up to death, and, rising from the dead, he destroyed death and restored life.

And that we might live no longer for ourselves but for him who died and rose again for us, he sent the Holy Spirit from you, Father, as the first fruits for those who believe, so that, bringing to perfection his work in the world, he might sanctify creation to the full.

He joins his hands and, holding them extended over the offerings, says:
P: Therefore, O Lord, we pray: may this same Holy Spirit graciously sanctify these offerings,

He joins his hands and makes the Sign of the Cross once over the bread and chalice together, saying:
P: that they may become the Body and Blood of our Lord Jesus Christ

He joins his hands.
P: for the celebration of this great mystery, which he himself left us as an eternal covenant.

For when the hour had come for him to be glorified by you, Father most holy, having loved his own who were in the world, he loved them to the end: and while they were at supper,

He takes the bread and, holding it slightly raised above the altar, continues:

P: he took bread, blessed and broke it, and gave it to his disciples, saying,

He bows slightly.

P: TAKE THIS, ALL OF YOU, AND EAT OF IT, FOR THIS IS MY BODY, WHICH WILL BE GIVEN UP FOR YOU.

He shows the consecrated host to the people, places it again on the paten, and genuflects in adoration. After this, he continues:

P: In a similar way,

He takes the chalice and, holding it slightly raised above the altar, continues:

P: taking the chalice filled with the fruit of the vine, he gave thanks, and gave the chalice to his disciples, saying:

He bows slightly.

P: TAKE THIS, ALL OF YOU, AND DRINK FROM IT, FOR THIS IS THE CHALICE OF MY BLOOD, THE BLOOD OF THE NEW AND ETERNAL COVENANT, WHICH WILL BE POURED OUT FOR YOU AND FOR MANY FOR THE FORGIVENESS OF SINS. DO THIS IN MEMORY OF ME.

He shows the chalice to the people, places it on the corporal, and genuflects in adoration. Then he says:

P: The mystery of faith.

C: We proclaim your Death, O Lord, and profess your Resurrection until you come again.

Or:

When we eat this Bread and drink this Cup, we proclaim your Death, O Lord, until you come again.

Or:

Save us, Savior of the world, for by your Cross and Resurrection you have set us free.

Then, with hands extended, the Priest says:

P: Therefore, O Lord, as we now celebrate the memorial of our redemption, we remember Christ's Death and his descent to the realm of the dead, we proclaim his Resurrection and his Ascension to your right hand, and, as we await his coming in glory, we offer you his Body and Blood, the sacrifice acceptable to you which brings salvation to the whole world.

Look, O Lord, upon the Sacrifice which you yourself have provided for your Church, and grant in your loving kindness to all who partake of this one Bread and one Chalice that, gathered into one body by the Holy Spirit, they may truly become a living sacrifice in Christ to the praise of your glory.

Therefore, Lord, remember now all for whom we offer this sacrifice: especially your servant N. our Pope, N. our Bishop, and the whole Order of Bishops, all the clergy, those who take part in this offering, those gathered here before you, your entire people, and all who seek you with a sincere heart.

Remember also those who have died in the peace of your Christ and all the dead, whose faith you alone have known. To all of us, your children, grant, O merciful Father, that we may enter into a heavenly inheritance with the Blessed Virgin Mary, Mother of God, with blessed Joseph, her Spouse, and with your Apostles and Saints in your kingdom. There, with the whole of creation, freed from the corruption of sin and death, may we glorify you through Christ our Lord, through whom you bestow on the world all that is good.

He takes the chalice and the paten with the host and, raising both, he says:

P: Through him, and with him, and in him, O God, almighty Father, in the unity of the Holy Spirit, all glory and honor is yours, for ever and ever.

C: Amen.

Then follows the Communion Rite.

THE COMMUNION RITES

After the chalice and paten have been set down, the Priest, with hands joined, says:

P: At the Savior's command and formed by divine teaching, we dare to say:

He extends his hands and, together with the people, continues:

Our Father, who art in heaven, hallowed be thy name; thy kingdom come, thy will be done on earth as it is in heaven. Give us this day our daily bread, and forgive us our trespasses, as we forgive those who trespass against us; and lead us not into temptation, but deliver us from evil.

With hands extended, the Priest alone continues, saying:

P: Deliver us, Lord, we pray, from every evil, graciously grant peace in our days, that, by the help of your mercy, we may be always free from sin and safe from all distress, as we await the blessed hope and the coming of our Savior, Jesus Christ.

He joins his hands. And the people conclude the prayer, acclaiming:

C: For the kingdom, the power and the glory are yours now and forever.

Then the Priest, with hands extended, says aloud:

P: Lord Jesus Christ, who said to your Apostles: Peace I leave you, my peace I give you; look not on our sins, but on the faith of your Church, and graciously grant her peace and unity in accordance with your will. Who live and reign for ever and ever.

C: Amen.

The Priest, turned towards the people, extending and then joining his hands, adds:

P: The peace of the Lord be with you always.

C: And with your spirit.

P: Let us offer each other the sign of peace.

Breaking of the Bread

Meanwhile the following is sung or said:

Lamb of God, you take away the sins of the world: have mercy on us.

Lamb of God, you take away the sins of the world: have mercy on us.

Lamb of God, you take away the sins of the world: grant us peace.

Then the Priest, with hands joined, says quietly:

P: Lord Jesus Christ, Son of the living God, who, by the will of the Father and the work of the Holy Spirit, through your Death gave life to the world, free me by this, your most holy Body and Blood, from all my sins and from every evil; keep me always faithful to your commandments, and never let me be parted from you.

Or:

P: May the receiving of your Body and Blood, Lord Jesus Christ, not bring me to judgement and condemnation, but through your loving mercy be for me protection in mind and body and a healing remedy.

The Priest genuflects, takes the host and, holding it slightly raised above the paten or above the chalice, while facing the people, says aloud:

P: Behold the Lamb of God, Behold him who takes away the sins of the world. Blessed are those called to the supper of the Lamb.

C: Lord, I am not worthy that you should enter under my roof, But only say the word and my soul shall be healed.

The Priest, facing the altar, says quietly:

P: May the Body of Christ keep me safe for eternal life.

And he reverently consumes the Body of Christ. Then he takes the chalice and says quietly:

P: May the Blood of Christ keep me safe for eternal life.

And he reverently consumes the Blood of Christ.

Communion

After this, he takes the paten or ciborium and approaches the communicants. The Priest raises a host slightly and shows it to each of the communicants, saying:

P: The Body of Christ.

The communicant replies:

C: Amen.

(And receives Holy Communion)

Prayer after Communion

When the distribution of Communion is over, the Priest or a Deacon purifies the chalice and the paten. While he carries out the purification, he says quietly:

P: What has passed our lips as food, O Lord, may we possess in purity of heart, that what has been given to us in time may be our healing for eternity.

Then, standing at the altar or at the chair and facing the people, with hands joined, the Priest says:

P: Let us pray.

The Priest, with hands extended, says the Prayer after Communion, at the end of which the people acclaim:

C: Amen.

THE CONCLUDING RITES

The Priest, facing the people and extending his hands, says:

P: The Lord be with you.

C: And with your spirit.

P: May almighty God bless you, the Father, and the Son, and the Holy Spirit.

C: Amen.

Dismissal

Then the Deacon, or the Priest himself, with hands joined and facing the people, says:

P: Go forth, the Mass is ended.

Or:

P: Go and announce the Gospel of the Lord.

Or:

P: Go in peace, glorifying the Lord by your life.

Or:

P: Go in peace.

C: Thanks be to God.

The congregation remains standing until the priest and the procession have left the church.

SECTION II

PREFACES OF HOLY MASS

PREFACE I OF ADVENT

It is truly right and just, our duty and our salvation, always and everywhere to give you thanks, Lord, Holy Father, almighty and eternal God, through Christ our Lord.

For he assumed at his first coming the lowliness of human flesh, and so fulfilled the design you formed long ago, and opened for us the way to eternal salvation, that, when he comes again in glory and majesty and all is at last made manifest, we who watch for that day may inherit the great promise in which now we dare to hope.

And so, with Angels and Archangels, with Thrones and Dominions, and with all the hosts and Powers of heaven, we sing the hymn of your glory, as without end we acclaim:

Holy, Holy, Holy Lord God of hosts…

PREFACE II OF ADVENT

It is truly right and just, our duty and our salvation, always and everywhere to give you thanks, Lord, Holy Father, almighty and eternal God, through Christ our Lord.

For all the oracles of the prophets foretold him, the Virgin Mother longed for him with love beyond all telling, John the Baptist sang of his coming and proclaimed his presence when he came.

It is by his gift that already we rejoice at the mystery of his Nativity, so that he may find us watchful in prayer and exultant in his praise.

And so, with Angels and Archangels, with Thrones and Dominions, and with all the hosts and Powers of heaven, we sing the hymn of your glory, as without end we acclaim:

Holy, Holy, Holy Lord God of hosts…

PREFACE I OF THE NATIVITY OF THE LORD

It is truly right and just, our duty and our salvation, always and everywhere to give you thanks, Lord, Holy Father, almighty and eternal God.

For in the mystery of the Word made flesh a new light of your glory has shone upon the eyes of our mind, so that, as we recognize in him God made visible, we may be caught up through him in love of things invisible.

And so, with Angels and Archangels, with Thrones and Dominions, and with all the hosts and Powers of heaven, we sing the hymn of your glory, as without end we acclaim:

Holy, Holy, Holy Lord God of hosts…

PREFACE II OF THE NATIVITY OF THE LORD

It is truly right and just, our duty and our salvation, always and everywhere to give you thanks, Lord, Holy Father, almighty and eternal God, through Christ our Lord.

For on the feast of his awe-filled mystery, though invisible in his own divine nature, he has appeared visibly in ours; and begotten before all ages, he has begun to exist in time; so that, raising up in himself all that was cast down, he might restore unity to all creation and call straying humanity back to the heavenly Kingdom.

And so, with Angels, we praise you, as in joyful celebration we acclaim:

Holy, Holy, Holy Lord God of hosts…

PREFACE III OF THE NATIVITY OF THE LORD

It is truly right and just, our duty and our salvation, always and everywhere to give you thanks, Lord, Holy Father, almighty and eternal God, through Christ our Lord.

For through him the holy exchange that restores our life has shone forth today in splendour: when our frailty is assumed by your word not only does human mortality receive unending honour but by this wondrous union we, too, are made eternal.

And so, in company with the choirs of Angels, we praise you, and with joy we proclaim:

Holy, Holy, Holy Lord God of hosts…

EPIPHANY OF THE LORD

It is truly right and just, our duty and our salvation, always and everywhere to give you thanks, Lord, Holy Father, almighty and eternal God.

For today you have revealed the mystery of our salvation in Christ as a light for the nations, and, when he appeared in our mortal nature, you made us new by the glory of his immortal nature.

And so, with Angels and Archangels, with Thrones and Dominions, and with all the hosts and Powers of heaven, we sing the hymn of your glory, as without end we acclaim:

Holy, Holy, Holy Lord God of hosts…

PREFACE OF LENT I

It is truly right and just, our duty and our salvation, always and everywhere to give you thanks, Lord, Holy Father, almighty and eternal God, through Christ our Lord.

For by your gracious gift each year your faithful await the sacred paschal feasts with the joy of minds made pure, so that, more eagerly intent on prayer and on the works of charity, and participating in the mysteries by which they have been reborn, they may be led to the fullness of grace that you bestow on your sons and daughters.

And so, with Angels and Archangels, with Thrones and Dominions, and with all the hosts and Powers of heaven, we sing the hymn of your glory as without end we acclaim:

Holy, Holy, Holy Lord God of hosts…

PREFACE OF LENT II

It is truly right and just, our duty and our salvation, always and everywhere to give you thanks, Lord, Holy Father, almighty and eternal God.

For you have given your children a sacred time for the renewing and purifying of their hearts, that, freed from disordered affections, they may so deal with the things of this passing world as to hold rather to the things that eternally endure.

And so, with all the Angels and Saints, we praise you, as without end we acclaim:

Holy, Holy, Holy Lord God of hosts…

PREFACE OF LENT III

It is truly right and just, our duty and our salvation, always and everywhere to give you thanks, Lord, Holy Father, almighty and eternal God.

For you will that our self-denial should give you thanks, humble our sinful pride, contribute to the feeding of the poor, and so help us imitate you in your kindness.

And so we glorify you with countless Angels, as with one voice of praise we acclaim:

Holy, Holy, Holy Lord God of hosts…

PREFACE OF LENT IV

It is truly right and just, our duty and our salvation, always and everywhere to give you thanks, Lord, Holy Father, almighty and eternal God.

For through bodily fasting you restrain our faults, raise up our minds, and bestow both virtue and its rewards, through Christ our lord. Through him the Angels praise your majesty, Dominions adore and Powers tremble before you.

Heaven and the Virtues of heaven and the blessed Seraphim worship together with exultation. May our voices, we pray, join with theirs in humble praise, as we acclaim:

Holy, Holy, Holy Lord God of hosts…

PREFACE I OF THE PASSION OF THE LORD

It is truly right and just, our duty and our salvation, always and everywhere to give you thanks, Lord, Holy Father, almighty and eternal God.

For through the saving Passion of your Son the whole world has received a heart to confess the infinite power of your majesty, since by the wondrous power of the Cross your judgment on the world is now revealed and the authority of Christ crucified.

And so, Lord, with all the Angels and Saints, we, too, give you thanks, as in exultation we acclaim:

Holy, Holy, Holy Lord God of hosts…

PREFACE II OF THE PASSION OF THE LORD

It is truly right and just, our duty and our salvation, always and everywhere to give you thanks, Lord, Holy Father, almighty and eternal God, through Christ our Lord.

For the days of his saving Passion and glorious Resurrection are approaching, by which the pride of the ancient foe is vanquished and the mystery of our redemption in Christ is celebrated. Through him the host of Angels adores your majesty and rejoices in your presence for ever.

May our voices, we pray, join with theirs in one chorus of exultant praise, as we acclaim:

Holy, Holy, Holy Lord God of hosts…

PREFACE I OF EASTER

This Preface is said at the Easter Vigil (on this night); *on Easter Sunday, and throughout the Octave of Easter* (on this day); *and other days of Easter Time* (in this time).

It is truly right and just, our duty and our salvation, at all times to acclaim you, O Lord, but (on this night / on this day / in this time) above all to laud you yet more gloriously, when Christ our Passover has been sacrificed.

For he is the true Lamb who has taken away the sins of the world; by dying he has destroyed our death, and by rising, restored our life.

Therefore, overcome with paschal joy, every land, every people exults in your praise and even the heavenly Powers, with the angelic hosts, sing together the unending hymn of your glory, as they acclaim:

Holy, Holy, Holy Lord God of hosts…

PREFACE II OF EASTER

The following Preface is said during Easter Time.

It is truly right and just, our duty and our salvation, at all times to acclaim you, O Lord, but in this time above all to laud you yet more gloriously, when Christ our Passover has been sacrificed.

Through him the children of light rise to eternal life and the halls of the heavenly Kingdom are thrown open to the faithful; for his Death is our ransom from death, and in his rising the life of all has risen.

Therefore, overcome with paschal joy, every land, every people exults in your praise and even the heavenly Powers, with the angelic hosts, sing together the unending hymn of your glory, as they acclaim:

Holy, Holy, Holy Lord God of hosts…

PREFACE III OF EASTER

The following Preface is said during Easter Time.

It is truly right and just, our duty and our salvation, at all times to acclaim you, O Lord, but in this time above all to laud you yet more gloriously, when Christ our Passover has been sacrificed.

He never ceases to offer himself for us but defends us and ever pleads our cause before you: he is the sacrificial Victim who dies no more, the Lamb, once slain, who lives for ever.

Therefore, overcome with paschal joy, every land, every people exults in your praise and even the heavenly Powers, with the angelic hosts, sing together the unending hymn of your glory, as they acclaim:

Holy, Holy, Holy Lord God of hosts…

PREFACE IV OF EASTER

The following Preface is said during Easter Time.

It is truly right and just, our duty and our salvation, at all times to acclaim you, O Lord, but in this time above all to laud you yet more gloriously, when Christ our Passover has been sacrificed.

For, with the old order destroyed, a universe cast down is renewed, and integrity of life is restored to us in Christ.

Therefore, overcome with paschal joy, every land, every people exults in your praise and even the heavenly Powers, with the angelic hosts, sing together the unending hymn of your glory, as they acclaim:

Holy, Holy, Holy Lord God of hosts…

PREFACE V OF EASTER

The following Preface is said during Easter Time.

It is truly right and just, our duty and our salvation, at all times to acclaim you, O Lord, but in this time above all to laud you yet more gloriously, when Christ our Passover has been sacrificed.

By the oblation of his Body he brought the sacrifices of old to fulfilment in the reality of the Cross and, by commending himself to you for our salvation, showed himself the Priest, the Altar and the Lamb of sacrifice.

Therefore, overcome with paschal joy, every land, every people exults in your praise and even the heavenly Powers, with the angelic hosts, sing together the unending hymn of your glory, as they acclaim:

Holy, Holy, Holy Lord God of hosts…

PREFACE I OF THE ASCENSION OF THE LORD

The following Preface is said on the day of the Ascension of the Lord. It may be said on the days between the Ascension and Pentecost in all Masses that have no proper Preface.

It is truly right and just, our duty and our salvation, always and everywhere to give you thanks, Lord, Holy Father, almighty and eternal God.

For the Lord Jesus, the King of glory, conqueror of sin and death, ascended (today) to the highest heavens, as the Angels gazed in wonder.

Mediator between God and man, judge of the world and Lord of hosts, he ascended not to distance himself from our lowly state but that we, his members, might be confident of following where he, our Head and Founder, has gone before.

Therefore, overcome with paschal joy, every land, every people exults in your praise and even the heavenly Powers, with the angelic hosts, sing together the unending hymn of your glory, as they acclaim:

Holy, Holy, Holy Lord God of hosts…

PREFACE II OF THE ASCENSION OF THE LORD

The following Preface is said on the day of the Ascension of the Lord. It may be said on the days between the Ascension and Pentecost in all Masses that have no proper Preface.

It is truly right and just, our duty and our salvation, always and everywhere to give you thanks, Lord, Holy Father, almighty and eternal God, through Christ our Lord.

For after his Resurrection he plainly appeared to all his disciples and was taken up to heaven in their sight, that he might make us sharers in his divinity.

Therefore, overcome with paschal joy, every land, every people exults in your praise and even the heavenly Powers, with the angelic hosts, sing together the unending hymn of your glory, as they acclaim:

Holy, Holy, Holy Lord God of hosts…

PREFACE I OF THE SUNDAYS IN ORDINARY TIME

It is truly right and just, our duty and our salvation, always and everywhere to give you thanks, Lord, Holy Father, almighty and eternal God, through Christ our Lord.

For through his Paschal Mystery, he accomplished the marvellous deed, by which he has freed us from the yoke of sin and death, summoning us to the glory of being now called a chosen race, a royal priesthood, a holy nation, a people for your own possession, to proclaim everywhere your mighty works, for you have called us out of darkness into your own wonderful light.

And so, with Angels and Archangels, with Thrones and Dominions, and with all the hosts and Powers of heaven, we sing the hymn of your glory, as without end we acclaim:

Holy, Holy, Holy Lord God of hosts…

PREFACE II OF THE SUNDAYS IN ORDINARY TIME

It is truly right and just, our duty and our salvation, always and everywhere to give you thanks, Lord, Holy Father, almighty and eternal God, through Christ our Lord.

For out of compassion for the waywardness that is ours, he humbled himself and was born of the Virgin; by the passion of the Cross he freed us from unending death, and by rising from the dead he gave us life eternal.

And so, with Angels and Archangels, with Thrones and Dominions, and with all the hosts and Powers of heaven, we sing the hymn of your glory, as without end we acclaim:

Holy, Holy, Holy Lord God of hosts…

PREFACE III OF THE SUNDAYS IN ORDINARY TIME

It is truly right and just, our duty and our salvation, always and everywhere to give you thanks, Lord, Holy Father, almighty and eternal God.

For we know it belongs to your boundless glory, that you came to the aid of mortal beings with your divinity and even fashioned for us a remedy out of mortality itself, that the cause of our downfall might become the means of our salvation, through Christ our Lord.

Through him the host of Angels adores your majesty and rejoices in your presence for ever.

May our voices, we pray, join with theirs in one chorus of exultant praise, as we acclaim:

Holy, Holy, Holy Lord God of hosts

PREFACE IV OF THE SUNDAYS IN ORDINARY TIME

It is truly right and just, our duty and our salvation, always and everywhere to give you thanks, Lord, Holy Father, almighty and eternal God, through Christ our Lord.

For by his birth he brought renewal to humanity's fallen state, and by his suffering, cancelled out our sins; by his rising from the dead, he has opened the way to eternal life, and by ascending to you, O Father, he has unlocked the gates of heaven.

And so, with the company of Angels and Saints, we sing the hymn of your praise, as without end we acclaim:

Holy, Holy, Holy Lord God of hosts…

PREFACE V OF THE SUNDAYS IN ORDINARY TIME

It is truly right and just, our duty and our salvation, always and everywhere to give you thanks, Lord, Holy Father, almighty and eternal God.

For you laid the foundations of the world and have arranged the changing of times and seasons; you formed man in your own image and set humanity over the whole world in all its wonder, to rule in your name over all you have made and for ever praise you in your mighty works, through Christ our Lord.

And so, with all the Angels, we praise you, as in joyful celebration we acclaim:

Holy, Holy, Holy Lord God of hosts…

PREFACE VI OF THE SUNDAYS IN ORDINARY TIME

It is truly right and just, our duty and our salvation, always and everywhere to give you thanks, Lord, Holy Father, almighty and eternal God.

For in you we live and move and have our being, and while in this body we not only experience the daily effects of your care, but even now possess the pledge of life eternal.

For, having received the first fruits of the Spirit, through whom you raised up Jesus from the dead, we hope for an everlasting share in the Paschal Mystery.

And so, with all the Angels, we praise you, as in joyful celebration we acclaim:

Holy, Holy, Holy Lord God of hosts…

PREFACE VII OF THE SUNDAYS IN ORDINARY TIME

It is truly right and just, our duty and our salvation, always and everywhere to give you thanks, Lord, Holy Father, almighty and eternal God.

For you so loved the world that in your mercy you sent us the Redeemer, to live like us in all things but sin, so that you might love in us what you loved in your Son, by whose obedience we have been restored to those gifts of yours that, by sinning, we had lost in disobedience.

And so, Lord, with all the Angels and Saints, we, too, give you thanks, as in exultation we acclaim:

Holy, Holy, Holy Lord God of hosts…

PREFACE VIII OF THE SUNDAYS IN ORDINARY TIME

It is truly right and just, our duty and our salvation, always and everywhere to give you thanks, Lord, Holy Father, almighty and eternal God.

For when your children were scattered afar by sin, through the Blood of your Son and the power of the Spirit, you gathered them again to yourself, that a people, formed as one by the unity of the Trinity, made the body of Christ and the temple of the Holy Spirit, might, to the praise of your manifold wisdom, be manifest as the Church.

And so, in company with the choirs of Angels, we praise you, and with joy we proclaim:

Holy, Holy, Holy Lord God of hosts…

PREFACE I OF THE MOST HOLY EUCHARIST

It is truly right and just, our duty and our salvation, always and everywhere to give you thanks, Lord, Holy Father, almighty and eternal God, through Christ our Lord.

For he is the true and eternal Priest, who instituted the pattern of an everlasting sacrifice and was the first to offer himself as the saving Victim, commanding us to make this offering as his memorial. As we eat his flesh that was sacrificed for us, we are made strong, and, as we drink his Blood that was poured out for us, we are washed clean.
And so, with Angels and Archangels, with Thrones and Dominions, and with all the hosts and Powers of heaven, we sing the hymn of your glory, as without end we acclaim:
Holy, Holy, Holy Lord God of hosts…

PREFACE II OF THE MOST HOLY EUCHARIST

It is truly right and just, our duty and our salvation, always and everywhere to give you thanks, Lord, Holy Father, almighty and eternal God, through Christ our Lord.
For at the Last Supper with his Apostles, establishing for the ages to come the saving memorial of the Cross, he offered himself to you as the unblemished Lamb, the acceptable gift of perfect praise.
Nourishing your faithful by this sacred mystery, you make them holy, so that the human race, bounded by one world, may be enlightened by one faith and united by one bond of charity.
And so, we approach the table of this wondrous Sacrament, so that, bathed in the sweetness of your grace, we may pass over to the heavenly realities here foreshadowed.

Therefore, all creatures of heaven and earth sing a new song in adoration, and we, with all the host of Angels, cry out, and without end we acclaim:

Holy, Holy, Holy Lord God of hosts…

PREFACE I OF THE BLESSED VIRGIN MARY

It is truly right and just, our duty and our salvation, always and everywhere to give you thanks, Lord, holy Father, almighty and eternal God, and to praise, bless, and glorify your name (on the Solemnity of the Motherhood / on the feast day / on the nativity / in veneration) of the Blessed ever-Virgin Mary

For by the overshadowing of the Holy Spirit she conceived your Only Begotten Son, and without losing the glory of virginity, brought forth into the world the eternal Light, Jesus Christ our Lord.

Through him the Angels praise your majesty, Dominions adore and Powers tremble before you. Heaven and the Virtues of heaven and the blessed Seraphim worship together with exultation. May our voices, we pray, join with theirs in humble praise, as we acclaim:

Holy, Holy, Holy Lord God of hosts…

PREFACE II OF THE BLESSED VIRGIN MARY

It is truly right and just, our duty and our salvation, to praise your mighty deeds in the exaltation of all the Saints, and especially, as we celebrate the memory of the Blessed Virgin Mary, to proclaim your kindness as we echo her thankful hymn of praise.

For truly even to the earth's ends you have done great things and extended your abundant mercy from age to age: when you looked on the lowliness of your handmaid, you gave us through her the author of our salvation, your Son, Jesus Christ, our Lord.

Through him the host of Angels adores your majesty and rejoices in your presence for ever. May our voices, we pray, join with theirs in one chorus of exultant praise, as we acclaim:

Holy, Holy, Holy Lord God of hosts…

PREFACE I OF THE APOSTLES

It is truly right and just, our duty and our salvation, always and everywhere to give you thanks, Lord, Holy Father, almighty and eternal God.

For you, eternal Shepherd, do not desert your flock, but through the blessed Apostles watch over it and protect it always, so that it may be governed by those you have appointed shepherds to lead it in the name of your Son.

And so, with Angels and Archangels, with Thrones and Dominions, and with all the hosts and Powers of heaven, we sing the hymn of your glory, as without end we acclaim:

Holy, Holy, Holy Lord God of hosts…

PREFACE II OF THE APOSTLES

It is truly right and just, our duty and our salvation, always and everywhere to give you thanks, Lord, Holy Father, almighty and eternal God, through Christ our Lord

For you have built your Church to stand firm on apostolic foundations, to be a lasting sign of your holiness on earth and offer all humanity your heavenly teaching.

Therefore, now and for ages unending, with all the host of Angels, we sing to you with all our hearts, crying out as we acclaim:

Holy, Holy, Holy Lord God of hosts…

PREFACE I OF SAINTS

The following Preface is said in Masses of All Saints, of Patron Saints and of Saints who are Titulars of a church, and on Solemnities and Feasts of Saints, unless a proper Preface is to be said. This Preface may be said also on Memorials of Saints.

It is truly right and just, our duty and our salvation, always and everywhere to give you thanks, Lord, Holy Father, almighty and eternal God.

For you are praised in the company of your Saints and, in crowning their merits, you crown your own gifts.

By their way of life you offer us an example, by communion with them you give us companionship, by their intercession, sure support, so that, encouraged by so great a cloud of witnesses, we may run as victors in the race before us and win with them the imperishable crown of glory, through Christ our Lord.

And so, with the Angels and Archangels, and with the great multitude of the Saints, we sing the hymn of your praise, as without end we acclaim:

Holy, Holy, Holy Lord God of hosts…

PREFACE II OF SAINTS

The following Preface is said in Masses of All Saints, of Patron Saints and of Saints who are Titulars of a church, and on Solemnities and Feasts of Saints, unless a proper Preface is to be said. This Preface may be said also on Memorials of Saints.

It is truly right and just, our duty and our salvation, always and everywhere to give you thanks, Lord, Holy Father, almighty and eternal God, through Christ our Lord.

For in the marvellous confession of your Saints, you make your Church fruitful with strength ever new and offer us sure signs of your love. And that your saving mysteries may be fulfilled, their great example lends us courage, their fervent prayers sustain us in all we do. And so, Lord, with all the Angels and Saints, we, too, give you thanks, as in exultation we acclaim:

Holy, Holy, Holy Lord God of hosts…

PREFACE I OF HOLY MARTYRS

The following Preface is said on the Solemnities and Feasts of Holy Martyrs. It may also be said on their Memorials.

It is truly right and just, our duty and our salvation, always and everywhere to give you thanks, Lord, Holy Father, almighty and eternal God.

For the blood of your blessed Martyr N., poured out like Christ's to glorify your name, shows forth your marvellous works, by which in our weakness you perfect your power and on the feeble bestow strength to bear you witness, through Christ our Lord.

And so, with the Powers of heaven, we worship you constantly on earth, and before your majesty without end we acclaim:

Holy, Holy, Holy Lord God of hosts…

PREFACE II OF HOLY MARTYRS

The following Preface is said on the Solemnities and Feasts of Holy Martyrs. It may also be said on their Memorials.

It is truly right and just, our duty and our salvation, always and everywhere to give you thanks, Lord, Holy Father, almighty and eternal God.

For you are glorified when your Saints are praised; their very sufferings are but wonders of your might: in your mercy you give ardour to their faith, to their endurance you grant firm resolve, and in their struggle the victory is yours, through Christ our Lord.

Therefore, all creatures of heaven and earth sing a new song in adoration, and we, with all the host of Angels, cry out, and without end we acclaim:

Holy, Holy, Holy Lord God of hosts…

PREFACE OF HOLY PASTORS

The following Preface is said on the Solemnities and Feasts of Holy Pastors. It may also be said on their Memorials.

It is truly right and just, our duty and our salvation, always and everywhere to give you thanks, Lord, Holy Father, almighty and eternal God, through Christ our Lord.

For, as on the festival of Saint N. you bid your Church rejoice, so, too, you strengthen her by the example of his holy life, teach her by his words of preaching, and keep her safe in answer to his prayers.

And so, with the company of Angels and Saints, we sing the hymn of your praise, as without end we acclaim:

Holy, Holy, Holy Lord God of hosts…

PREFACE OF HOLY VIRGINS AND RELIGIOUS

The following Preface is said on the Solemnities and Feasts of Holy Virgins and Religious. It may also be said on their Memorials.

It is truly right and just, our duty and our salvation, always and everywhere to give you thanks, Lord, Holy Father, almighty and eternal God.

For in the Saints who consecrated themselves to Christ for the sake of the Kingdom of Heaven, it is right to celebrate the wonders of your providence, by which you call human nature back to its original holiness and bring it to experience on this earth the gifts you promise in the new world to come.

And so, with all the Angels and Saints, we praise you, as without end we acclaim:

Holy, Holy, Holy Lord God of hosts…

COMMON PREFACE I

The following Preface is said in Masses that have no proper Preface, and for which a Preface related to a specific liturgical time is not indicated.

It is truly right and just, our duty and our salvation, always and everywhere to give you thanks, Lord, Holy Father, almighty and eternal God, through Christ our Lord.

In him you have been pleased to renew all things, giving us all a share in his fullness. For though he was in the form of God, he emptied himself and by the blood of his Cross brought peace to all creation. Therefore he has been exalted above all things, and to all who obey him, has become the source of eternal salvation.

And so, with Angels and Archangels, with Thrones and Dominions, and with all the hosts and Powers of heaven, we sing the hymn of your glory, as without end we acclaim:

Holy, Holy, Holy Lord God of hosts…

COMMON PREFACE II

The following Preface is said in Masses that have no proper Preface, and for which a Preface related to a specific liturgical time is not indicated.

It is truly right and just, our duty and our salvation, always and everywhere to give you thanks, Lord, Holy Father, almighty and eternal God.

For in goodness you created man and, when he was justly condemned, in mercy you redeemed him, through Christ our Lord. Through him the Angels praise your majesty, Dominions adore and Powers tremble before you. Heaven and the Virtues of heaven and the blessed Seraphim worship together with exultation.

May our voices, we pray, join with theirs in humble praise, as we acclaim:

Holy, Holy, Holy Lord God of hosts…

COMMON PREFACE III

The following Preface is said in Masses that have no proper Preface, and for which a Preface related to a specific liturgical time is not indicated.

It is truly right and just, our duty and our salvation, always and everywhere to give you thanks, Lord, Holy Father, almighty and eternal God.

For just as through your beloved Son you created the human race, so also through him with great goodness you formed it anew.

And so, it is right that all your creatures serve you, all the redeemed praise you, and all your Saints with one heart bless you.

Therefore, we, too, extol you with all the Angels, as in joyful celebration we acclaim:

Holy, Holy, Holy Lord God of hosts…

COMMON PREFACE IV

The following Preface is said in Masses that have no proper Preface, and for which a Preface related to a specific liturgical time is not indicated.

It is truly right and just, our duty and our salvation, always and everywhere to give you thanks, Lord, Holy Father, almighty and eternal God.

For, although you have no need of our praise, yet our thanksgiving is itself your gift, since our praises add nothing to your greatness, but profit us for salvation, through Christ our Lord.

And so, in company with the choirs of Angels, we praise you, and with joy we proclaim:

Holy, Holy, Holy Lord God of hosts…

COMMON PREFACE V

The following Preface is said in Masses that have no proper Preface, and for which a Preface related to a specific liturgical time is not indicated.

It is truly right and just, our duty and our salvation, always and everywhere to give you thanks, Lord, Holy Father, almighty and eternal God, through Christ our Lord.

His Death we celebrate in love, his Resurrection we confess with living faith, and his Coming in glory we await with unwavering hope. And so, with all the Angels and Saints, we praise you, as without end we acclaim:

Holy, Holy, Holy Lord God of hosts…

COMMON PREFACE VI

The following Preface is said in Masses that have no proper Preface, and for which a Preface related to a specific liturgical time is not indicated.

It is truly right and just, our duty and our salvation, always and everywhere to give you thanks, Father most Holy, through your beloved Son, Jesus Christ, your Word through whom you made all things, whom you sent as our Saviour and Redeemer, incarnate by the Holy Spirit and born of the Virgin.

Fulfilling your will and gaining for you a holy people, he stretched out his hands as he endured his Passion, so as to break the bonds of death and manifest the resurrection.

And so, with the Angels and all the Saints, we declare your glory, as with one voice we acclaim:

Holy, Holy, Holy Lord God of hosts…

PREFACE I FOR THE DEAD

The following Preface is said in Masses for the Dead.

It is truly right and just, our duty and our salvation, always and everywhere to give you thanks, Lord, Holy Father, almighty and eternal God, through Christ our Lord.

In him the hope of blessed resurrection has dawned, that those saddened by the certainty of dying, might be consoled by the promise of immortality to come.

Indeed for your faithful, Lord, life is changed not ended, and, when this earthly dwelling turns to dust, an eternal dwelling is made ready for them in heaven.

And so, with Angels and Archangels, with Thrones and Dominions, and with all the hosts and Powers of heaven, we sing the hymn of your glory, as without end we acclaim:

Holy, Holy, Holy Lord God of hosts…

PREFACE II FOR THE DEAD

The following Preface is said in Masses for the Dead.

It is truly right and just, our duty and our salvation, always and everywhere to give you thanks, Lord, Holy Father, almighty and eternal God, through Christ our Lord.

For as one alone he accepted death, so that we might all escape from dying; as one man he chose to die, so that in your sight we all might live for ever.

And so, in company with the choirs of Angels, we praise you, and with joy we proclaim:

Holy, Holy, Holy Lord God of hosts…

PREFACE III FOR THE DEAD

The following Preface is said in Masses for the Dead.

It is truly right and just, our duty and our salvation, always and everywhere to give you thanks, Lord, Holy Father, almighty and eternal God, through Christ our Lord.

For he is the salvation of the world, the life of the human race, the resurrection of the dead.

Through him the host of Angels adores your majesty and rejoices in your presence for ever.

May our voices, we pray, join with theirs in one chorus of exultant praise, as we acclaim:

Holy, Holy, Holy Lord God of hosts…

PREFACE IV FOR THE DEAD

The following Preface is said in Masses for the Dead.

It is truly right and just, our duty and our salvation, always and everywhere to give you thanks, Lord, Holy Father, almighty and eternal God.

For it is at your summons that we come to birth, by your will that we are governed, and at your command that we return, on account of sin, to that earth from which we came.

And when you give the sign, we who have been redeemed by the Death of your Son, shall be raised up to the glory of his Resurrection. And so, with the company of Angels and Saints, we sing the hymn of your praise, as without end we acclaim:

Holy, Holy, Holy Lord God of hosts…

PREFACE V FOR THE DEAD

The following Preface is said in Masses for the Dead.

It is truly right and just, our duty and our salvation, always and everywhere to give you thanks, Lord, Holy Father, almighty and eternal God.

For even though by our own fault we perish, yet by your compassion and your grace, when seized by death according to our sins, we are redeemed through Christ's great victory, and with him called back into life.

And so, with the Powers of heaven, we worship you constantly on earth, and before your majesty without end we acclaim:

Holy, Holy, Holy Lord God of hosts…

Printed in Great Britain
by Amazon